To: _____

From: _____

Other books by Gregory E. Lang:

Why a Daughter Needs a Dad

Why a Son Needs a Dad

Why I Love Grandma

Why I Love Grandpa

Why a Son Needs a Mom

Why a Daughter Needs a Mom

Why I Chose You

Why I Love You

Why I Need You

Why We Are a Family

Why We Are Friends

Brothers and Sisters

Simple Acts

Love Signs

Life Maps

Thank You, Mom

· 100 Reasons Why I Am Grateful for You ·

GREGORY E. LANG

CUMBERLAND HOUSE

NASHVILLE, TENNESSEE

THANK YOU, MOM
PUBLISHED BY CUMBERLAND HOUSE PUBLISHING, INC.
431 Harding Industrial Drive
Nashville, TN 37211

ISBN-13: 978-1-58182-599-2
ISBN-10: 1-58182-599-4

Cover design: JulesRulesDesign
Cover photograph: GettyImages
Text design: Lisa Taylor
Interior photographs: Gregory E. Lang

Printed in Canada
1 2 3 4 5 6 7 8 — 12 11 10 09 08 07

To Mom—thank you for everything.

INTRODUCTION

I have much to be thankful for—the love and support of my family, my health, my many friends, my creature comforts, and more. Sometimes I am led to step back and assess how my life has unfolded. It is in those moments of introspection that I fully appreciate the help I've had from my family, friends, mentors, and advisors along every step of my life's journey. Equally important is what my parents gave me: a solid foundation on which to grow and learn. That foundation—the one my mother helped provide me—is what this book is about.

I have grown increasingly thankful for my mom as the years have gone by, especially now that, as a parent myself, I truly understand what is required to set into place all the building blocks necessary to support and nurture a child for a lifetime. With this book I hope I begin to take account of and adequately thank my mom for all she did to make sure I had a happy childhood. She worked hard to make sure I received the support and opportunities that made possible the fulfilling life I've led. Simply put, she helped me to thrive and enjoy myself.

The things my mother has done for me over the years are indeed numerous, and regrettably I'm sure I can't recall them all no matter how hard I might try. Yet I do have quite a few favorite "Mom" memories. For example, when I was a boy, every day began with a hot breakfast; she made sure I was dressed for the weather; she checked over my homework; she tended to my heart and flesh wounds with the same gentle loving care; and she cheered for me from the bleachers of every single one of my baseball games. I always got the birthday or Christmas present I wanted most, and my pestering, precocious questions were always answered. Mom taught me to ride a bicycle, manage a budget, mend a garment, cook my favorite foods, change a diaper, and years later, how to understand what my own infant needed when she cried.

Today, little has changed; when I visit she still offers a hot breakfast, fusses at me if she thinks I'm not dressed warmly enough for winter's chill, and sends me a birthday gift even though I've asked her not to spend the money. If she hears even a hint of a question I might have, she calls me with information she has found on the Internet or mails newspaper clippings she thinks may help. She offers me her secret recipes or cherished keepsakes and photographs from her childhood, and she still helps me to understand my child, now a teenager, when I can't see or comprehend what seems so obvious to a mom.

Of all the gifts, loving gestures, sweet reassurances, and life lessons I could thank my mother for, the one thing I think means the most to me, and for which I am immeasurably grateful, is really quite simple—she's never stopped being a mom. I can always count on my mom to be a good mother to me, as well as to my siblings. Her maternal nature carries over to how she acts as a grandmother; as I watch her with my child, I am reminded of how well she treated me.

There are, I think, a few universal hallmarks of a good parent: unconditional love, unfailing support, endless affection, and concern. These are the hallmarks of my mother. These are the characteristics that distinguish her in my heart and mind. These are the reasons I love her so much.

Although now older and less spry, her eyes and smile still offer reassurance and evidence of pride whenever she looks at me, as does the gentle touch she gives while listening intently to whatever it is I want to get off my chest. Her laughter still warms, as does her heartfelt embrace or the "How are you?" that welcomes me each time we see each other or talk on the phone. She would still drop everything to come to my aid if I needed her or cook a meal for me if I asked for it.

Even though I now recognize the countless things my mother did for me and I attempt in these pages to express my gratitude for them, the truth is when I was young I rarely showed appreciation for what she did for me. I simply did not say "thank you" when I should have. Maybe I was naïve, oblivious to the tasks and challenges of parenting, or just thought I was entitled to good treatment. But no matter what the excuse or belated confession, the fact remains my mother did what she did with little reward at the time. Albeit late and thankfully before I have regrets that I never told her, the time for her reward has come.

So here I am, all these years later, writing this book to say, "Thank you, Mom." With it I recognize and acknowledge the many sacrifices she made on my behalf and the caring gestures she has extended to me for more than forty-six years. In these pages I tell her, "I can't possibly thank you enough for everything you did, but I'm going to try." Even so, the expressions of gratitude that follow, whether simple, silly, or profound, are only the beginning of what I want to say to my mom and what I believe other children, young and old, want and should say to theirs. To that end, I have provided space for you to write your own personal message of thanks in the last pages of this book.

I believe a child cannot express enough gratitude for what a mother has done. I know that I cannot, but I also know my mother will be delighted I gave it a try. I love you, Mom, and thank you so very much for everything.

THANK YOU, MOM

Thank you, Mom, for

always making time to play with me on cold and rainy days.

■   ■   ■   ■   ■   ■   ■

Thank you, Mom, for

teaching me how to cook my favorite foods.

■   ■   ■   ■   ■   ■

Thank you, Mom, for . . .

not letting me grow up too fast.

all those times you tucked me in
at night with a kiss.

helping me to understand why I can't always have my way.

Thank you, Mom, for . . .

giving me the time and space

to become independent.

not expecting me to be perfect.

helping me to take care of the things

I couldn't handle by myself.

Thank you, Mom, for

taking me places to explore the wonders of the world.

■   ■   ■   ■   ■   ■   ■

Thank you, Mom, for

making sure we spent time together as a family.

■   ■   ■   ■   ■   ■

Thank you, Mom, for . . .

always showing your pride in me.

driving carpool for all those school
and summer activities.

making sure I learned to understand and respect "no."

Thank you, Mom, for . . .

making me learn to eat the yucky stuff
I didn't want to ever see again.

making sure my toys were safe
for me to play with.

making sure I knew how to act around strangers.

Thank you, Mom, for

not letting me take myself too seriously.

Thank you, Mom, for . . .

those braces, even though I hated them at the time.

starting my college fund as soon as you did.

loving me so much when it didn't seem
I loved you at all.

giving me all the opportunities you could.

Thank you, Mom, for

making sure I did my homework.

■   ■   ■   ■   ■   ■

Thank you, Mom, for . . .

being someone I could always count on.

holding me close when I needed
your comfort.

making sure I didn't get too spoiled.

Thank you, Mom, for

teaching me how to prepare for a job interview.

■   ■   ■   ■   ■   ■

Thank you, Mom, for

indulging each and every one of my hobbies.

■   ■   ■   ■   ■   ■

Thank you, Mom, for

helping me always look my best.

■　　　■　　　■　　　■　　　■　　　■

Thank you, Mom, for

protecting me from the dangers I couldn't see.

■   ■   ■   ■   ■   ■

Thank you, Mom, for . . .

explaining everything I needed to know

about the birds and the bees.

*teaching me how to conduct myself in
relationships with family and friends.*

teaching me to share my time as well as my things.

teaching me to take pride in all my endeavors.

Thank you, Mom, for . . .

not freaking out when I was learning to drive.

requiring me to respect authority
and teaching me when to question it.

helping me to understand the opposite sex.

making sure I learned and used good manners.

Thank you, Mom, for

all those long, long talks we've had.

■   ■   ■   ■   ■   ■

Thank you, Mom, for

allowing me to have the pets I wanted.

■   ■   ■   ■   ■   ■

Thank you, Mom, for

making my boo-boos feel better.

Thank you, Mom, for

letting me get to know who you really are.

■   ■   ■   ■   ■   ■

Thank you, Mom, for . . .

making sure I didn't eat too much junk food.

making sure I followed all the doctor's

and dentist's instructions.

making sure I didn't skip my naps.

not giving me an embarrassing nickname.

Thank you, Mom, for

making sure I made the best use of my talents.

■   ■   ■   ■   ■   ■   ■

Thank you, Mom, for

reassuring me when I doubted myself.

■   ■   ■   ■   ■   ■

Thank you, Mom, for

never failing to make me feel special to you.

■   ■   ■   ■   ■   ■

Thank you, Mom, for . . .

not putting up with my misbehavior.

indulging my sometimes strange selection of friends.

never seeming disappointed with the way
I've turned out.

not tolerating laziness and apathy in me.

Thank you, Mom, for

making sure I always had someone to play with.

■　　　■　　　■　　　■　　　■　　　■

Thank you, Mom, for

reading to me, even after I could read to myself.

■　　　■　　　■　　　■　　　■　　　■

Thank you, Mom, for

pushing me to do the things I didn't want to do
but needed to do.

Thank you, Mom, for . . .

forgiving me for all the stress

I'm sure I caused you.

making sure I really did slow down
and smell the roses.

praising me when I accomplished something important to me.

admitting when you were wrong;

it taught me character.

Thank you, Mom, for

always accepting the affection I wanted to give you.

Thank you, Mom, for

all the sacrifices you made to give me
the best life you could.

■   ■   ■   ■   ■   ■

Thank you, Mom, for

being the kind of parent I could look up to.

■   ■   ■   ■   ■   ■

Thank you, Mom, for

allowing me to grow up, even when you thought
you weren't ready for it.

Thank you, Mom, for

keeping a youthful spirit; it made you fun to be around.

Thank you, Mom, for

helping prepare me to leave home.

■   ■   ■   ■   ■   ■

Thank you, Mom, for . . .

showing me a better way when I did something wrong.

not taking embarrassing
photographs of me.

teaching me how to be a good spouse and parent.

Thank you, Mom, for

expecting my best but not pushing me beyond my capabilities.

Thank you, Mom, for

accepting there are some things about me
that are different from you.

Thank you, Mom, for . . .

helping me to understand the significance

of current events.

making sure I was always a good sport,
win or lose.

teaching me how to deal diplomatically with

prejudice and discrimination.

teaching me to give of myself more than I take from others.

Thank you, Mom, for

always being ready to catch me should I fall.

■   ■   ■   ■   ■   ■

Thank you, Mom, for

listening intently to what I was trying to say.

Thank you, Mom, for

keeping a watchful eye on me.

■   ■   ■   ■   ■   ■

Thank you, Mom, for . . .

teaching me how to swim.

teaching me how to resist peer pressure.

not allowing me to smoke and use drugs.

expecting me to be a good and responsible employee.

Thank you, Mom, for

being patient with me when I was impatient with you.

Thank you, Mom, for

caring for my pets even though I said I would do everything.

■   ■   ■   ■   ■   ■   ■

Thank you, Mom, for . . .

forgiving my infractions but holding me accountable for them.

showing me how to plan and live

within a budget.

showing me how to do my own laundry.

Thank you, Mom, for

helping me judge what is important and what's not.

■   ■   ■   ■   ■   ■   ■

Thank you, Mom, for

helping me find myself.

■　　■　　■　　■　　■　　■

Thank you, Mom, for

teaching me how and when to ask for help.

■   ■   ■   ■   ■   ■

Thank you, Mom, for . . .

always coming when I called for you, and for coming even
when I didn't think I needed you.

encouraging me to use my imagination.

giving me your affection, even when
I didn't seem to want it.

Thank you, Mom, for . . .

making sure I stayed healthy.

setting limits on me when I needed them.

being the beacon of hope for our family.

Thank you, Mom, for

telling me so often that you love me.

■   ■   ■   ■   ■   ■

Thank you, Mom, for

expecting me to be gracious when others
were generous toward me.

■ ■ ■ ■ ■ ■

Thank you, Mom, for

all those times you hugged me for no reason.

■   ■   ■   ■   ■   ■

Thank you, Mom, for

everything I can think of, for all those things I'm sure
I have forgotten about, and especially
for those things I never knew you did for me.

Paste your picture here and
write your reason
on the opposite page.

Thank you, Mom, for

_____

ACKNOWLEDGMENTS

A book about giving thanks to parents would not be complete without also giving thanks to my Heavenly Father. I confess, I sometimes succumb to human nature and think to myself it was my research, talent, and perseverance that resulted in my success as an author. The truth is, however, years ago I was lost and in despair, and I had not an ounce of experience in creative writing. One evening in a prayer I asked for help and then did my best to go forward with hope. Soon certain events began to transpire—like a friend telling me of a successful little book that eventually inspired me to write; my introduction to Janet Lankford-Moran, the photographer who helped me complete my first book; meeting Ron Pitkin, my publisher, who coincidentally, but not known to me until later, was the publisher of the successful little book that got me started in the first place; and then there are all those events in my life that have been the fabric with which my stories about love, faith, forgiveness, and duty are woven. And now my book about thanks, the only one that has closed with a testimonial such as this, is in your hands. Coincidence? Serendipity? Chance? I think not. I once was lost, but now I'm found. Thank you, God.

TO CONTACT THE AUTHOR

write in care of the publisher:
Cumberland House Publishing
431 Harding Industrial Drive
Nashville, TN 37211

or e-mail the author:
greg.lang@mindspring.com

visit the author's Web site:
gregoryelang.com